I Ain't a Lecturer:
by J-Zone

"Everybody dies on this muthafuckin' album."

Words of wisdom from Spice 1, one of the masters of what the media dubbed "gangsta rap," also known as "hardcore rap," "street rap," and everybody's favorite, "reality rap." The coloring book you've just bought is dedicated entirely to the pioneers and current baton holders of the world's most misunderstood subgenera. You coulda bought a Hardy Boy's mystery or an Agatha Christie novel, dummy. Well, now that we're rollin' on 43-inch rims at your expense, you might as well get some history.

"When I wrote about parties, it didn't fit..."

Words of wisdom from the one Ice-T, a pioneer of the West Coast Gangsta rap scene. His smash hit "6 In Tha Morning" was one of the tracks that set the foundation for this style of rap. Instead of rockin' parties, these dudes were robbin' 'em. Instead of doin' the hustle, they rapped about hustlin'. Instead of callin' the police to secure the disco, these dudes were sayin' "Fuck Tha Police!" They ducked bullets while others danced to "Rapper's Delight." So rappin' about shit they'd never own over a disco break was a moot point when they dealt with triflin' shit on a daily basis. Brains were splattered on tape, hookers were blasted on record, the word "bitch" was used with the frequency of a Foxxy Brown brand-name mention, the word "ho" was NEVER to be used to refer to a garden tool, and cussin' was like breathin'.

Some artists were just havin' fun with it and signifyin'. Just talkin' some shit in a Dolemite/Blowfly fashion. Some used extreme graphic rhymes and angst to speak out against what Middle America was too wrapped up watching *Cheers* to notice. To some, it was just expression of what they saw; but the less talented of this genre over-flooded the market and created a backlash, fucking it up for some of the more talented artists.

"...Now that we're rollin' on 43-inch rims at your expense, you might as well get some history."

Some people, who were pop-rap artists, got a "gangsta" edge back in 1993, 'cause gangsta rap had officially taken over. Onyx on the east, Death Row in the west, Geto Boys and Poison Clan in the south. Masta Ace's brilliant 1993 *Slaughtahouse* LP and Black Sheep's 1991 *Wolf In Sheep's Clothing* both humorously poked fun at the genre that had become a mockery of itself. But there are a few tasteless people like myself that actually find bad, generic, poorly produced gangsta rap albums enjoyable in a twisted sort of way. True, these "bad apples" could also be considered an addition to the genocide that "the system" really wants.

Yes, I'm pretty sure the artists didn't mean for their records to seem funny. But sometimes, you gotta laugh at the cartoonish violence, excessive profanity, and poor sound quality on Master P's *Mama's Bad Boy* LP or nod furiously to the funky and controversial St. Ides Malt Liquor commercials of the early 90s. Even though you know St. Ides might one day put your dick in a sling and probably kill your sperm cells quicker than Nonoxyl-9, those commercials are a hot property today because of their heavy wit and high funk factor.

It's too easy to just shake your head in disgust 'cause while some of the music was a lame knock-off of itself, at least some of it was hilarious and downright funky.

Some "gangsta" rap albums are rap classics (i.e. most NWA-related, Rap-A-Lot, Compton's Most Wanted, X-Raided, Death Row, Ice-T, Mob Style, and Schoolly D records). Some are just funny and truly tasteless, and some are just run-of-the-mill, but at last we'll give light to each and every artist who made an impact on this subgenera. Some of the selections I agree with, some I don't, but fuck all this shit talkin' – I ain't a lecturer.

Word.

SCHOOLLY D

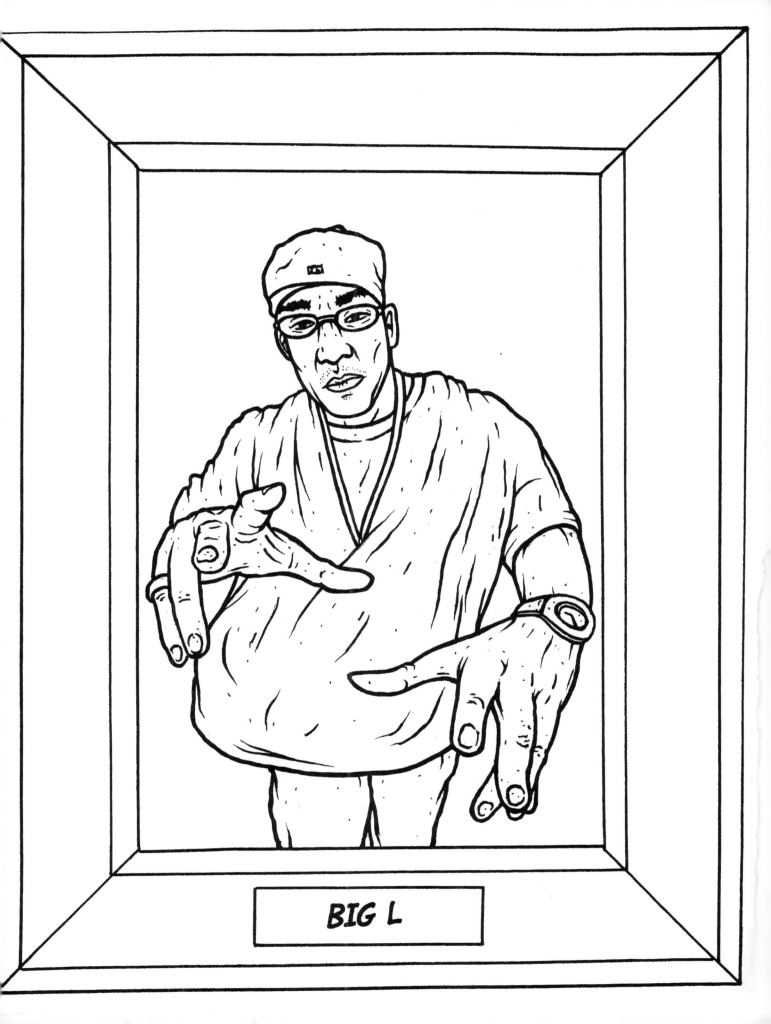

BIG L

NOTORIOUS B.I.G.

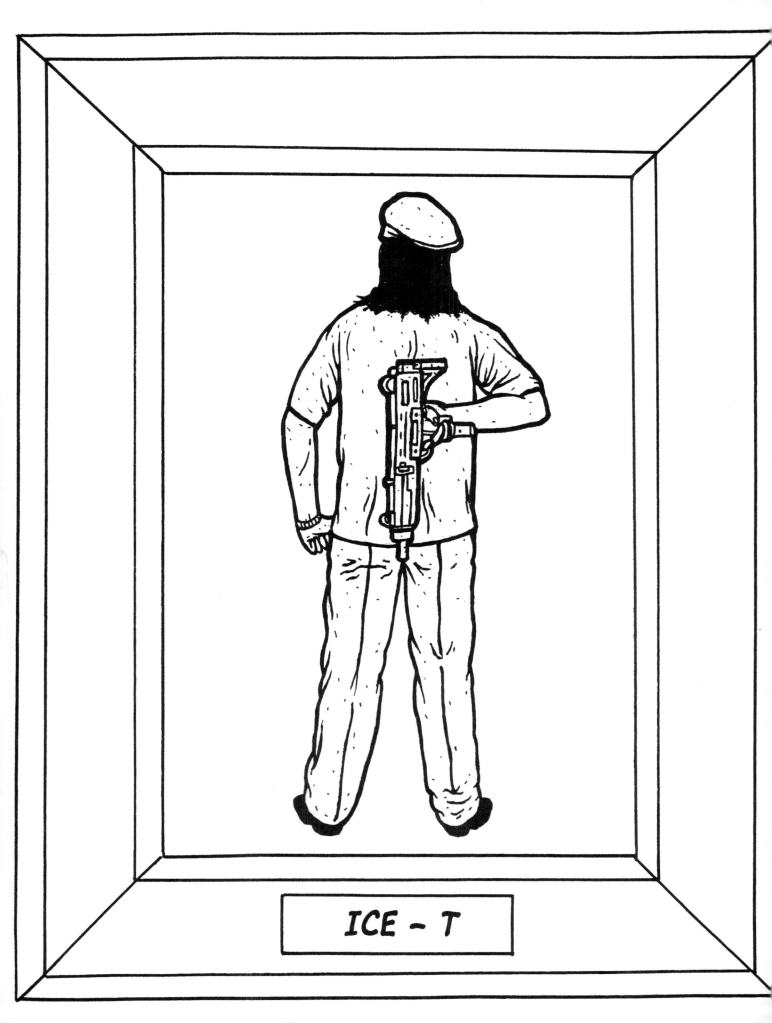

ICE - T

SCARFACE

E-40

TRICK DADDY

BROTHA LYNCH HUNG

NATE DOGG

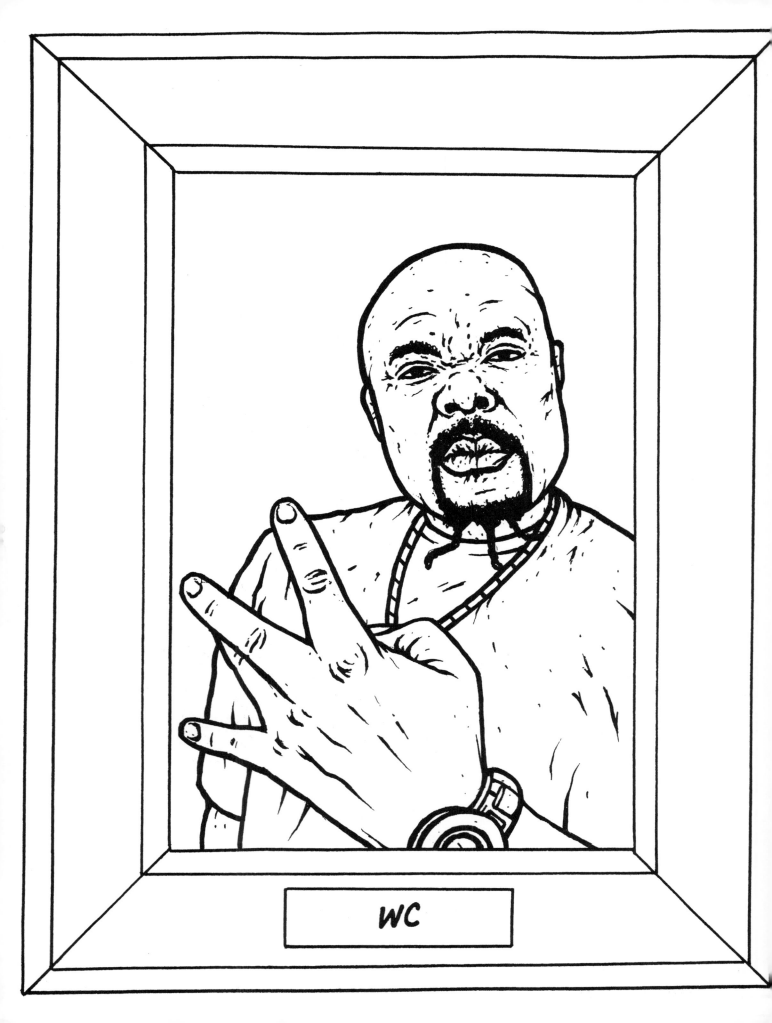

WC

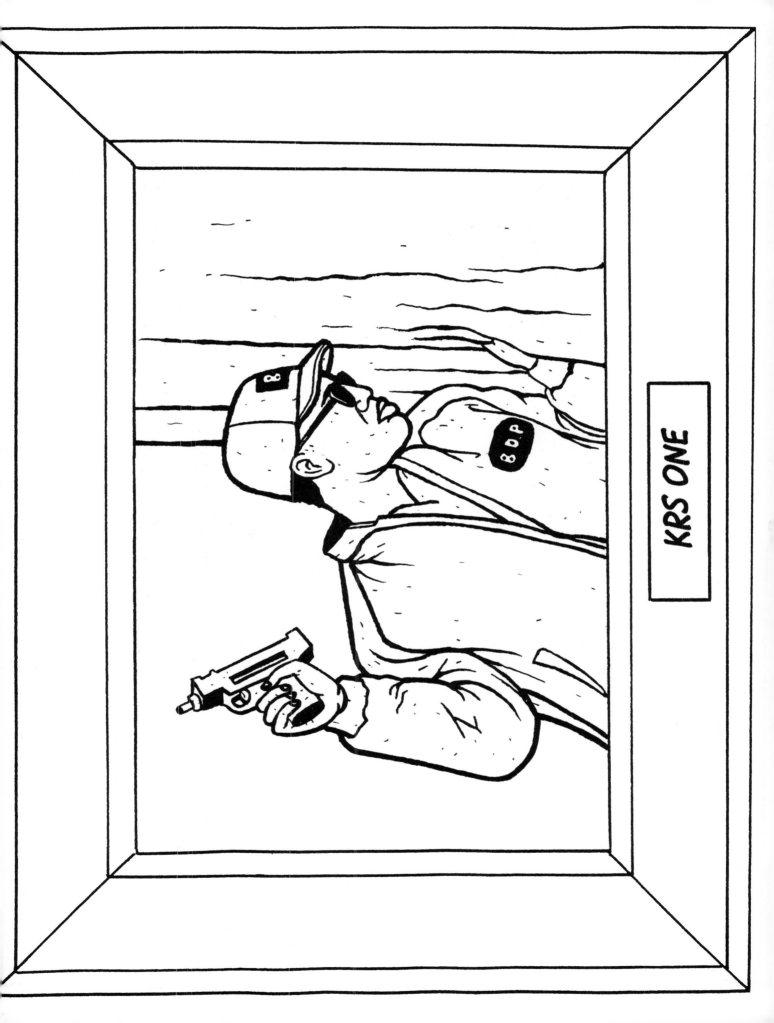

KRS ONE

DJ QUIK

DJ SCREW

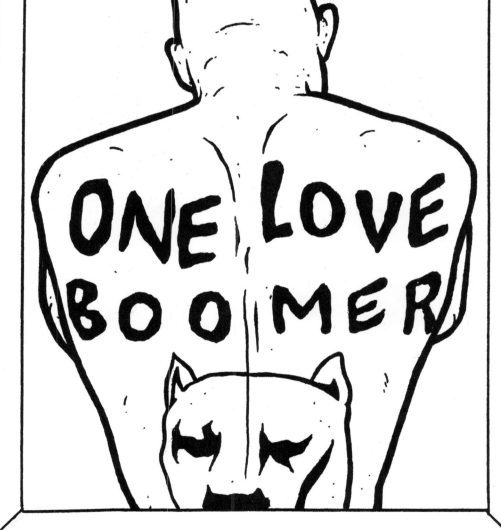

DMX

ESHAM

50 CENT

SUGE KNIGHT

MASTER P

KING TEE

KID FROST

CYPRESS HILL

MACK 10

MOBB DEEP

MC REN

SPICE 1

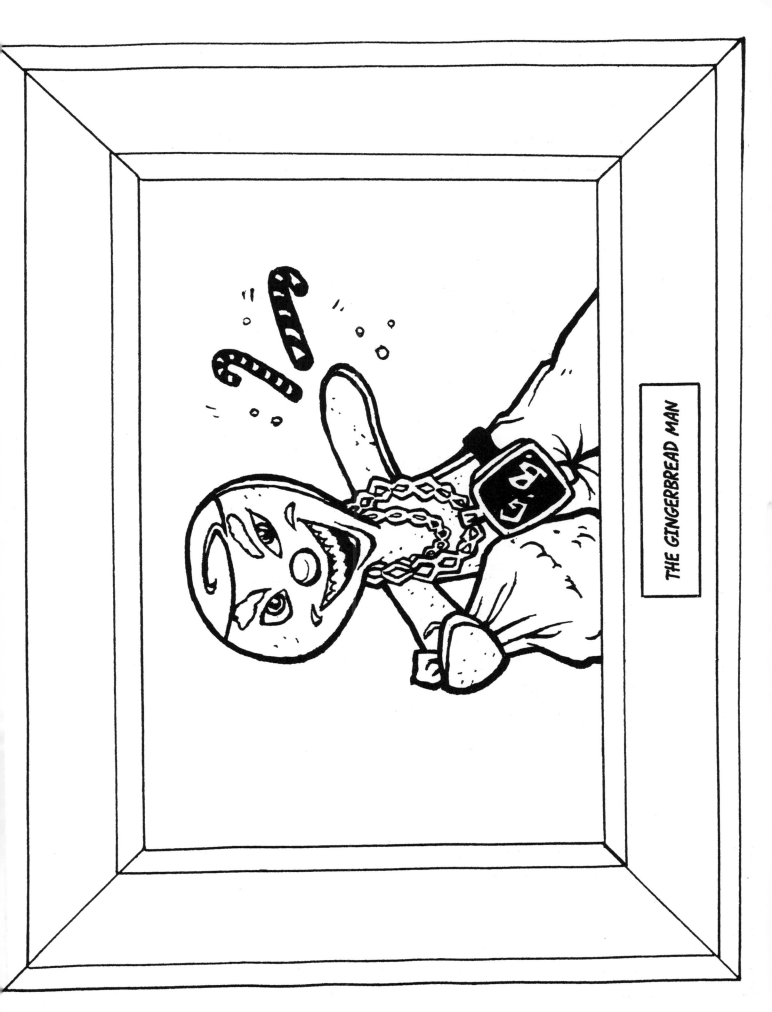

THE GINGERBREAD MAN

ICE CUBE

DR. DRE

ABOVE THE LAW

EAZY E

SNOOP DOGG

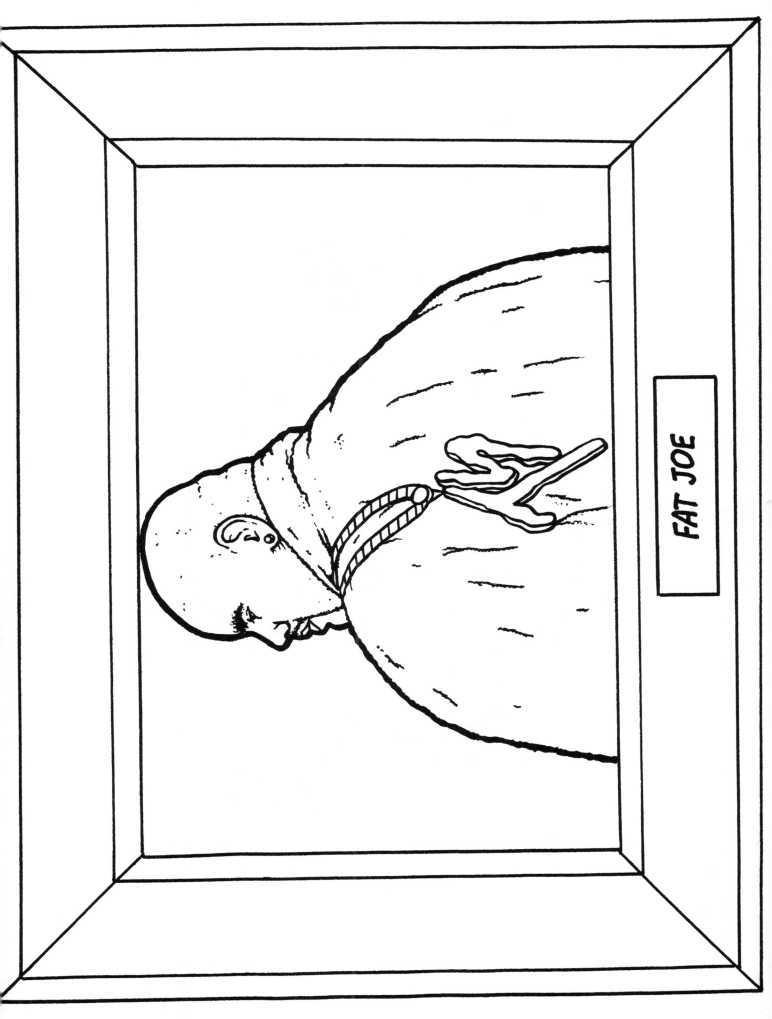

C-BO

TOO $HORT

MC EIHT

DRAW YOUR OWN GANGSTA RAP SUPERSTAR HERE

Color Within the Lines: An Afterword
by Sacha Jenkins

Gangsta rappers need love too, and they get it and give it all the same, just like the rest of us do. Still, many of us like to colour them bad, which is why our friend Aye Jay's *Gangsta Rap Coloring Book* is like, stupid fresh. And so what could be more better than drawing your very own man in black; filling him full with the robust flavors that light our lives? Yeah. Better yet, to quote the great forgotten, early '90s pranksta rap troupe Son of Bazerk, "What could be better, bitch?"

Dr. Dre of NWA and Snoop Dogg / Dre solo fame is a splendid West Coast gangsta. He used to rock Raiders' caps while he and his crew busted caps on wax. **Ice-T**—yet another fine Westside ruffian fortified with gritty street tales and busty beauties on his 12 inches—really got/gets down for his crown, pimp. Let's face it, a lot of these gangsta's are from the wild wild West: there's the aforementioned **Snoop**, the Long Beach Commissioner of banger cool, there's **MC Eiht**, a straight G who spells his name without a "g" (which is rather gangsta). Yea, plenty left coasters, but we can't forget an intelligent East Coast hoodlum like the South Bronx's very own Kris **"KRS ONE"** Parker or Philadelphia's Jesse **"Schoolly D"** Weaver—the angel-dust smoking Parkside Killer. Alotta people wanna argue about where the whole gangsta rap thing originated, but man, I just say worry about the Crayolas. Just pretend that the *Gangsta Rap Coloring Book* is one lovely coast...a coast where the coast is filled with creative rage, and the coast is always clear and free from bullets (unless we're talkin' lyrical bullets like the ones fired through the teefus of South Bronx ruffian **Tim** "Fuck Compton" **Dog**).

One coast, one love, true, but the California love must continue: **Gingerbread Man** is a mystery, but he's been spotted in the Bay Area with Z-Man from Hiero Imperium Records; **Too Short**—a legend looming atop cheeba clouds since the early '80s—*IS* the Yay Area, a mack who, even though he's bounced out to the more comfy pastures of Hotlanta, continues to have a stranglehold on those who walk

the streets of San Francisco and Oaktown; **2Pac**, our beloved black Elvis, a figure bigger than rap itself, a thespian and a gangsta on levels that Nelson George hasn't even had time to figure on just yet; **Ice Cube**, former partner of West Coast Dr. Dre and DJ Yella and MC Ren and the G in the sky **Eazy E**...a thespian, like Pac, and gangsta rap's first Walter Chronkite; **Kid Frost**, the biggest kid you've ever seen with the illest Chicano gangsta lean; **King Tee**'s flows defied region, even as he walked down back alleys in Compton or Watts with actual fucking crazy long guns in his hand (ask Glen E. Friedman—he took the flicks).

> *"Alotta people wanna argue about where the whole gangsta rap thing originated, but man, I just say worry about the Crayolas."*

How about Bay guardian **E-40**? Now, well, *wow*: his slanguage arts are superiorly thuggish on the outside, Pablo Piccaso-ish on the inside. They also will melt in anyone's mouth who isn't him. Down South, grimy Houston G's like the **Geto Boys** (Willie "clean up man" D, Mr. Mr. Scarface and Lord Bushwick Bill, y'all) always knew how to tell stories like they've been doing behind bars for centuries. **Brotha Lynch Hung** is the man who pioneered the "rip gut" steezo of gangsta flows (kudos). **Fat Joe**—yet another portly Latino hardass—is best known for sharing the realities of his native South Bronx, New York, with those of us who don't know (go to the BX and ask fools about Joey Crack; the streets will say things).

DJ Screw went from the South to parts way North (waaaay North— Rest in peace, bruh), and he's taken his syrupy, dying battery stylings with him (keep trying, suckas). **WC** is the ultimate "check 'yo self before I check you outta this life" emcee (make sure your shit is on point before you have anything to say about this man. And definitely don't C.R.I.P. walk if you ain't got no business doing it...). **50 Cent** is Amerika's gangsta pinup of the decade; he's made bullet holes sexy. His raps are often violent and cathartic all the same!

Who else? Yea, **Tha Dogg Pound** Gangsta's (peace

Daz Dillinger, peace Kurrupt and crew unnamed) have always been ready for war (even if they're warring amongst themselves. Guess that's a West Coast thang). **MC Ren**? What more can I say? OK, I'll say it: NWA. Brownsville, Brooklyn's Mash Out Posse (AKA **M.O.P.**, AKA Billie Danze and Lil' Fame) ain't nothin' to fuck with.

Dogs are loyal friends 'til the end. **Nate Dogg**, a preacher's son, has been loyal to this gangsta shit since day one. **Mack 10**, still another Westie, forever has a scowl on his face. **C-Bo** was jailed when his raps were considered a parole violation! Queensbridge's **Mobb Deep** have been known to shoot people, sometimes at the offices of prominent management companies...**Freddie Foxxx**: nobody wants it with Freddie Foxxx. You want his gangsta music and you want to be scared, but you don't want to get hurt in real time. Which is a serious possibility when it comes to the triple X. **DJ Quik** has always had good hair, great beats and even greater mack/trigger friendly raps. **Kool G Rap**, some might say, is the very best. The best G, at least, ever to kick complex flows through one veil of a lisp. **Spice 1**: best stutter-stepping gangsta flows. **Master P**: best gumbo-tinged gangsta grunts.

More dogs: **DMX** is the most passionate gangsta ever to bark on the mic—dead or alive. And then there's **Esham**, who has sorta always been on some Satan-type shit—which might be scary—but you've gotta peep the long running relationship between hell and tha blooze (which explains why we sometimes have sympathy for the devil). **Trick Daddy** has the best teeth ever. If Luke Campbell was a born again gangsta, Trick Daddy is who he'd aim to one day be.

Suge Knight. You know the drill. Definitely color within the lines, kids. For real.

Harlem's **Big L** was the Devil's son long before Nas became God's son...**Cypress Hill** be the type of dudes who could just kill a man—a feeling that most of us just don't understand. **Notorious B.I.G.** sold crack on the corner around the corner from where I live now (actually, I live around the corner from the corner where *he* used to slang crack. Who the fuck do I think I am?). **Bone Thugs** really are thuggish— I've seen it first hand, in Cleveland. I done seen many guns and other things, too.

Scarface. Again. Gets propers as a solo gangsta who loves KISS (and claims to have been in the KISS Army as a kid)! **Above the Law**: funky mathematicians with mad love for the number 187 (jeah, and you don't stop). And last, but not least, we've got the Big Easy's **Hot Boys** crew. The good people down New Orleans way are really into sprinkling the hell sauce all over their foods, so probably Crayola-ing these cats in flaming Tabasco orange would be a sure fire hit.

Word.

AYE JAY'S THANK YOUS:

Meka, Cohen, and Greta; Larry & Lucretia Klungtvet; the Moranos; the Melcons; the Sagers; the Fickens; everyone at Last Gasp—especially Ron, Anna, Colin, & Bucky; J-Zone & the Old Maid Billionaires; Sacha Jenkins & *Ego Trip*; Shepard Fairey, Amanda Fairey, & Studio Number One; Mike Patton; Ian Mackaye; Schoolly D; hip hop photographers – especially Glen E. Friedman; Heathakilla; Matt Loomis; E.J.; Faydog; J-Gold; Sacred Hoop (Luke Sick, Vrse Murphy, & DJ Marz); G-Pek; Eddie K; Z-Man; Mike 2600 & Burlesque Design; A. Horkey & Doug Surreal (Jack Spaar); DJ Quest; Eddie Def; Wez & *Lifesucksdie* magazine; Deejay Oh; Max; Bill; Spencer & the *Synthesis*; Paradise Lost Video; Peter Agoston & Culturama/Female Fun Records; Jacob Honan; Ron Dare; Chen Compton; Brandon B & gametightelectro; AWOL One; Mr.Dibbs; Lyrics Born; Lydia & Quannum; Queen Latifah; Mark & Future Primitive Sound; Mark Dancey & *Motorbooty* magazine; Dalek; Live Human; Todd & Consolidated; Bigfoot; Teenage Millionaire; Kevin & *Gum* magazine; Barry McGee; Mike & Lewis Recordings; Girlie Action; Dave Kinsey; Oliver Wang; Henry & *Chunklet* magazine; Turntable Lab; Hiphopsite; TRC; Dusty Groove; Red Five; Aquarius Records; Chris & Groove Merchant; Noah & *Mass Appeal*; P Minus & ATAK; the *News & Review*; Victoria & *So Graham Norton*; Mike & *Elemental*; Brian & *Mesh* magazine; *Jane*; *Black Book*; *Thrasher*; *Anthem*; *V*; *Grand Slam*; *Urb*; *Murder Dog*; the *Forecast*; *Vibe*; *XLR8R*; *GQ*; the *Face*; the City of Chico; and anyone who I may have forgotten. Thanks again...